Passed Away of A Sun

Arlington National Cemetery
Arlington, Virginia, USA
Poetic Novel

Please take a moment to look, reflect upon your life as you view
(pause, reflect) before you read
'Passed Away of a Sun.'

Written by Carol Lee Brunk

Passed Away of a Sun

DEDICATION

To all those who made Life possible and make Life possible today!

Carol Lee Brunk
Independent Educator Contractor
www.sightwordsataglance.com
Email: carol.brunk@yahoo.com
Cell: 224-239-9877

Self-published publication
Published in the United States

CONTENTS

Passed Away of a Sun

DESCRIPTION WITH BLESSING

This is a poetic short novel from a civilians view while looking at Arlington National Cemetery, Arlington, VA

The Riddle?
What happen to those addressed in arced stone?
Mystery to be told or never know?

Blessings to those that sleep in the grounded permanent beds and to those that survive to keep life to living for present for the unending of the promised tomorrow. Of the covenant, the rainbow still arises in the sky. God's blessing to all.

HISTORY POETRY COMMENTARY BY THE AUTHOR

American history class can record a time and teach a time era, period, event and the seconds on a clock but it can Not tell you everything that happened to an individual that passed away to keep life living to present day due to war or war of the world. You yourself alive do Not know, if what they are experiencing sleeping in the permanent ground, that you can consciously tell those that you stand upon or before their cemented grave arc in the cemetery to tell them life survived to their face and hug them for a life died to up hold life to live for all the world. Then tell them they are Not 'Jesus Christ' as noted to many times by those with lack of respect for a religion. *Religion under attack as well as the individual to know that all can be identified as a war weapon or used by an individual as a war weapon.* Those that use it against others by oneself or others use it to not have to explain an alternate directive or direction. Most often a power play to get one self or themselves where they want to be or others in life.

You pray with prayers for blessings to be heard to bless them (the passed away) for peace they should have experienced here without ever lying to sleep in permanent ground. Peace experience on earth breathed in without experienced horror until they passed away.

To solve and ponder a riddle in each grave arced of stone. In 'Passed Away of the Sun' each chapter starts with a stand of a visit to the cemetery. In that stand a view of observation of each grave stone in Arlington National Cemetery. Of one standing before with clear visual of the arced grave stones, a person's thought pattern rambles, rolls, searches for an answer to try to identify what happened to all those according to the time period of war written on an arced grave stone. Each paragraph written is a separate thought pattern combined with other thought patterns of perspective others involved in a situation or situations during a moment in passing in the time of war. In lieu of each grave stone you stand before, a grave stone marker marks the separate thought pattern(s) in each paragraph that one stand before the grave stone may experience with feet planted firmly in the direction of a flag so honored in the distance that flies a mixed colored hue pigmented rectangular designed flapping at times stagnate of air space traveled. You, the witness, of testimony within the Arlington National Cemetery, the testimony of the graved marked was placed with honor and promise for a better future to be held to uphold a growing countries political doctrines to preserve, maintain with the promise the fight held. The fight held for the future to survive. Life to survive.

The wars so far noted in 'Passed Away of the Sun' are

Chapters 1,2,3,4, 5

World War I 1914-1918 (more than 9 million military, 7 million civilians dead, End of War deaths estimated total on oppositions 5,525,000 opposed to 4,386,000 =   mostly due to technology advances) **4 YEARS OF WORLD KILLING**

World War II 1939-1945 (100 million people involved over 30 countries, military deaths estimated 21-25 million dead, December 7, 1941 Pearl Harbor death totaled 2,403 dead, the mass deaths of civilians including Holocaust was estimated to be 11 million, Hiroshima and Nagasaki , **end of war results estimated 50-85 million dead worldwide) 6 YEARS OF WORLD KILLING**

Vietnam 1955-1975 (South Vietnam, South Korea, United States, Australia, New Zealand, Thailand, Philippines deaths totaled 479,660 opposition to North Vietnam, North Korea, Soviet Union, China deaths totaled 455,476, **end of war results estimated 935,136** Note: 19 year war Only part of some of the reasons that a lower death total than World War II was due to the entrance of year into the war by each country.
19 YEARS OF KILLING

Gulf War – Operation Desert Sands 1990-1991 (Oil War) (148 US soldiers, 145 non-hostiles, 200 Kuwait, 20,000-35,000 frontline/reserve troops, 1,000 Kuwait civilians, 3664 Iraqi civilians additional 300 other civilians killed total **end of war death estimated total 40,457** (estimated total includes 35,000 instead of 20,000 for frontline/reserve) **1 YEAR OF KILLING**

References:
www.wikipedia.com for historical death (fatalities), American History classes that include high and college courses that also included Art History, American Literature, news releases that include Time magazine and other magazines, Television, newspapers, etc. See footnotes or additional references.

Please take a moment to look, reflect upon your life as you view (pause, reflect) before you read

'Passed Away of a Sun'...

1ST CHAPTER

The black passed away a dawning of a new day raised the shine away with brightness of celebration of a clear sparkling white – clouds that puff a smoke of the same color of a man blowing the rings that strengthened - a result of an elongated cigar. A judgment that was won to rest upon a gavel as it hit the bench. The décor was supreme. A repeat of a gavel hitting mahogany wood. A moment again, as the ring of puff of white exhale from the same color of the man- no grey of temple at the sides to ever hear as years never appear. God's grant of age of a seat that only reflects knowledge and not of a man's independent soul. God's grace placed in between the sentences of a passed judgment – a relief of a beginning that man stepped a continued forward as he climbs the steps to another gavel to hit the mahogany bench of a disappearance only to reflect in a passing that a crocheted blanket warmth or not may rest in the chair. In the opposition selected chair by the final gavel hit is the end of the end-not a rest for the peace for those in place upon the grey cemented arcs in green but absent the name of the opposition chair to a heavenly host. Even though the gavel hits the preexistence of the others arced passed of the oppositions chair greetings of hugs to hold – No War but two fingers vivid in the air upon the clouds they rest. Fine-tuned from cables, wires, metal colander

1

hats with many prongs that are not of rinsing of harvest gardens, moved to a drip line or a clear chemical of odor that put an eternity of eternal combustion upon an opposition that the gavel stayed firm to rest in place- the sound to those in clear view a recall final end of end.

Of no more passing of a passerby viewing that stands firm to a view that valleys and raises cemented arcs, back stretched to strength firmness of a wish, as the side of the palm lifts from above the brow in forward movement it lays to rest. *Commentary of 'I'll do my best...' When will it be marked completely filled of end of end?'* Hoping there would never be a next time.

Arms that can hold- are barren- no response from above for the vacancy that holds for those that wait to see those that had been saluted that day. Where's the vacancy? Heart. She's still waiting and so is he. That wasn't the return. Shredded paper from the mill colored from dyes of root, soil of the earth and flower's pigmented hue bottled where absorbed. The paper bundles held high. Small amounts tied in paper bags. The wedding gown waits in the parlor of the church it draped of the train, it travels out of the closet. She's awake. Takes her shower. Starts for the beginning of a day that will last- a hopeful day. Hands were held. The summer's warmth soiled the crease in the clothes where the arms where attached. The sun held high holding the heat wave. A summer's day had it passed?

Monumental holdings that had been established held the ground firm once attended by both. The days travel in the direction – questioned the welcome. Arced in view the preview. *'They are there for a purpose,"* commentary in the whirl of out stretched travels that passed the trees – the clear view faster than recorded from visual at one angle- human angle in a straight ahead position that can't be redirected in a flash- it was too fast.

Arc's rolled though they held its place- they held their own. Was it a mile? The stretch in view. The blades are green that sprout from the ground – no blood visual. A remembrance of a day that had *None*- when and where they stood before the return of a new stoned arc permanent residence addressed accordingly name inscribed- addressed with no rent or postage stamp – no charge.

He's got his hand with hers and introductions where made. *"How long has it been?"* they milled in conversation. The sky blue that day in more colors than they would had imagined before their arrival. "Where or whom where the guests?" was the comment while the travels out of town took them away. They milled in conversation standing in the untouched green that did not blade through the travels that the arced had taken on introductions and the wonder *'Who was the guest(s)'? Or who were the guest(s)?*

"Pass the oats that was stirred on an open fire." The freshness churned the stomach to a delightful state- a calming that filled in every taste. God listened to the fold and pressed hands together after and before a middle yellowing hit. God granted a prayer. The sides chosen different- values the same.

Sands, greenery thick-hard to slice the solid. A mixture of- *'Can I hide in wearing a visual?' "How's the sun glasses?' the commentary.* His conversations full of weighted pitch to the ears had two behind the line waiting for the arc to be filled- not knowing.

Introductions continued in span placement of ink on wood that was applied thinly to make a resemblance in 3-d-pictorial. Lain in for the present and the former-captions held a head line in both and all places. A record that is recorded for the life and lives placed- cold stone informed of present and past. The look for...*'When did it happen?" "What did they tell you?" was the commentary.* It was their arrival that the uniform appearance now entered into a familiar scene- too many doors that were knocked upon. Breathe held both sides of the door the opening glance- a diet had been issued to take the collapse of weight all felt at the simultaneous moment-*What was prescribed?*

Clouds that never miss a day – a flight that was an ending or a beginning entrance to the top with a glance backward in climb the visual closed box or unique vase that contains both labeled one- decorated with the fabricated hues that where never to be replaced with a different pigmentation – the standing free flight in a breeze representation of social written order- the plight to flight *FREE-*the trees bow at the days – greetings made.

'Sign on the dotted line.' 'Was it dotted?-I don't' remember?' the *commentary ensued.* What was issued in transportation chosen by few or many? Trucks that wheels rotated more through terrain- how fast? Was it planned? -When the papers were issued. The conversation: *'My kid's two teeth are missing.' 'Got a new picture?'* The commentary that Mother dropped the glass soiled a cloth with milk- any child would have loved that puddle to clean-the craving for spilt milk.

1st Chapter

History commentary:

Phrase: **'Spilt Milk'** Meaning: WITHOUT war the everyday aches, pains, crabbiness, normal, silly complaints that do not cause war or cause a monopoly of unfortunate happenings to oneself or others that include a headache from the seasonal fields of sinus allergy relieved by a shower of rain to rinse the pollen away or another example I don't feel like doing that and the only thing that happens is you put the laundry off till the next day. Common everyday complaints without dismemberment, guns shot in the face, a physical attack that includes paranoia just to get through to another day to stay physically alive for yourself and others.

Please take a moment to look, reflect upon your life as you view (pause, reflect) before you read *'Passed Away of a Sun'*...

2ND CHAPTER

We stood here before. Only this time the weather warmed the day. *'Memories 'Do they match yours?' slight commentary while they gazed upon the arced that cemented their existence that they stood for all of us.* 'My neighbors in there?' 'Did he ever get married?' commentary.* It's the step upon another step. The youth projected forward the past in the future. Love thy "My ONLY'- be true- wait. Palms placed smaller to older the same in status- in gender are both opposite and the same. *'A hand off on the trail 'Was it cold that day?' the commentary.* The run may have been miles that morning – 'what metal took place?' Was it not written down for visual appearance for the past to future?'*

'How long has it been?' 'Any news?' the commentary. The box empty again. Hoping lost postage of a stamp was the reason. I needed to talk, to pray. Written words were delivered. Knowing your still hoping that visual sight has a feel to it. A physical return- a journey's end of what end?

Oil refined. Olive's name changed for a different reason. Its relative thickness pushed for transportation. Of earth bound vegetable or mineral. 'Was there enough to spread around?' the commentary. Stock and stockings on hold- the bare essentials fashioned the name plate. Flour, butter, milk added to heated temperature juice of the meat-stirred- it created the gravy. *'How do we cook that again?' commentary.*

Of the winds that blew and blow' the smoke stacks piled the fluff – only the manufacturer knew- the industry. *'The cigar has been lit,'' the commentary.* The match lit the way- how much light did they need any way? The crack of light thundered power arrival by man or God or both. Percussion, the echo drum had results negative, positive or both. *'Hold your gut.' 'Helps on the way!' commentary.* The triathlon had a new name Survival. The sweat of moisture was heated to a temperature. *'Water for the thirst' 'And the smell' the commentary.* The rains of moisture became the common bath for the body not just for nature.

Weddings planned a year in advance. The flight to plight resulted in an overnight year in advance. *'I wore my mother's gown' the commentary.* Alterations sped up time from the past to present. *'Luck had it- it was a perfect fit' the commentary.* The needle and thread was Not removed from the sewing basket that day. Bouquets grabbed as the walk out the door with a convenient vase-the grab was made in the hall way. Fabric'd flowers! "The KISS" held host on the page in return.

Eyes opened. The distraught look-helplessness in groups. *'How thin were they?' 'I saw skeletons in biology class that looked better' the commentary.* Decompossion filled the air. Massive burial happened. Some were lucky to be sent home The plots thickened or was it expanded in an arced plot where they added the address and dressed décor fabric of a bed of permanent sleep *'My Uncle's in there' the commentary.* Camp got a negative name- the marshmallows that made S'mores never happened. Was the chocolate bar in the package? Did it ever arrive?

'Snows melted' 'Not ready for the day' the commentary. Was the time behind when things happen for a reason or not? 'There are blisters on my heals that haven't healed' 'What about your heart?' the commentary. Seasons changed habits as people change habits. Weathering the storm may not have happened

for the after storm pick up. The lightening damage hitting the tree incinerated-only a bare spot shown –was or where's the-remains. Winds that blow in the other direction changes direction-*Will the same things travel the path in a travel back? 'Have the geese migrated yet?' the commentary.* Home.

Warmth of the hands firmly held each other's then their own was sought in their absence-many times over. *'Your neck tie." "Let me help you securing it firmly' the commentary. 'I think I have the flu' 'It's really hard to breath' the commentary.* They did not have to turn around – knowing what was hanging. Boy scouts had the triple knots tied badges earned – what happen when something hung without praise? *'I pounded the steaks.' 'Till they are* tender' *the commentary.* Ground animals found the holes much more at home. The arc of grey cemented the earth in more than an area that was marked with an address labeled in stone. A send-off prayer for a white dove to land looking for a covenant hoping to land would never end. The words for a rescue could not be uttered in words or thoughts that show on a physical hope- holding out for the absence of hope. Praying for the sun to rise again. God was written to more times a day without a pencil, pen or writing tool of any kind.- it was displayed upon their physical strength. *'Where was the bathroom, again?' 'With the delicate paper décor'd walls?' the commentary.* The mirror was never to be shown or displayed in that shape or frame.

"Bon Voyage" should always have a positive send off to a positive return. A plus of an inevitable addition to family one may have been the nine months. The other may be minus a few that others carried the nine months instead of an adoption of an unplanned package number more than twins that equaled to different nations looking for the life saver instead of a pacifier replaced -the bottle. The floatation of a device may have been used for the good and the bad unknowingly.

"Knowledge" that goes without the passing is found in fossilized rock close to complete decomposition of ever knowing what it was originally. The collapse of weight upon the ground produces the sound that needed to be quiet – a disturbance- the last crunch before silence. *What did it cost you? Me? The*

others that will never know? Who heard it besides the weighted collapse of the deliverer- the halo was waved over.

'Newspaper!' the commentary was yelled. It was supposed to be a daily event in the morning. 'What's the date of the paper?' 'Can you recall?' the commentary. When the attic smell is delivered at what point of time and by whom? As the trucks passed cranking at high speed to the sound of silence that waits. The dry wall was supposed to be taken down at the time of renovation or a natural disaster – the unplanned wasn't what was to be expected nor was the crawl spaces- the laundry chute got a different name at times and so did the chimney- a prayer they did not light a fire.

'I'll meet you at the top of the stairs,' the commentary. The stair climb of leaps, springs, the skip of a step to a step of a stone's throw lake, river or pond- the creeks would happen after an intense rain or was it reign or an attics door hinge in time. 'I was looking for the skip of a step at the top of the stairs,' the commentary. 'Not an advance look into the clouds where the son illuminates to a point of No return decent,' the commentary.

Maps are a display of geography traveled or to travel. Directions more than once the destination looks completely different while traveling directly through the fireworks-cancelled during the sendoff – a hold off until the holiday of a celebration occurrence or can occur.

Shovels – a small garden. Houzed a home security to a rest. The dirt was removed by shovel full- to plant or was it hide the seed –NO need to replace the shoveled full that hid LIFE. Sanded Storms of yellow sand lay upon the winds of yesterday. 'Did your uniform match?' the questioned commentary.

'I lay awake at night.' 'Because I can't sleep,' the commentary. It wasn't the insomnia that kept me awake or lack of exercise-the preferred alternative. Thoughts of dreams of having a dream was discussed in a place that should have been a flight booked for a vacation in the distant future- Not a surprise

8

destination in time not disclosed by either side. What was in the surprise? My eyes are in the blind fold- Where was the party piñata? Talking became minimal to the point of a gesture – No words or nothing just follow the person in front of you. I wasn't looking for the exit out of Life door that may be behind them or anything else.

'How many days did it rain?' 'It wasn't 40?' 'Was it?' the commentary. *'How many days without rain' 'It wasn't 40?' 'Was it?' the commentary. 'I was advised to wear NO tattoos of religion though it's my religious freedom,' the commentary.* Safety was a prime concern- especially when you forfeit a humanitarian right without being informed in advance- defensive to the opposite to survive. The Ten in the Old Testament rang in but demand proved to be the positive in the opposite for survival.

'Not like the old westerns the fastest gun in the West,' the commentary. *'There was 'No Lone Rangers.'* Horses traded in for metal was not the electronic bull in a bar. Zoom! Zoom! Rotation of two to four or more in wheels roved. Thirsty quench for breathe happened more often in a shortened run for a life or your own. The band aide box was attached to a 24 hour nurse that prayed for cognitive activity and response-if you maid the stretcher. The aches that include those of distance traveled included a heart ache in both places. A reminder that a person will be there when the return happens – the live for a memory of a departure already taken place in time.

Monopoly, Pay Day, Sorry, Candy Land, Connect 4, Mystery Date, Checkers, Chess, UNO, Poker, Crazy 8, Go Fish, Battle Ship the games where of the future of a past board that did not mean bored that should have never left the contained box in the altered state but were only to be kept on a shelf for a rival of a holiday past- they were only to be played on the rested table without a gray cemented arc constantly anticipated by others around or those that were not in view.

2nd *Chapter*

'Did you fly the flag?' *'I wore it for you without the half mast,'* the commentary. *'The cemented arc is delayed.'*

History commentary Bible:

2 Corinthians 5:13

13 'If we are out of our mind, it is for the sake of God; if we are in our right mind, it is for you."

Please take a moment to look, reflect upon your life as you view (pause, reflect) before you read *'Passed Away of a Sun'*...

3RD CHAPTER

The elongated cigar waited, it smoldered with more all across the continents, the waiting took place as silence typed away. It was the elevation that occurred – the drawers flung open. Hands to hands grabbed the contents of the polar cold, who were the heroes in silence that were not identified? Hands grabbed, charges pressed, life went a different travel as hands grabbed, who would or will survive? The redness of sweat and the calmness of the cold chilled waiting to detour at any moment. The brass burned in more than one way on both sides the anger brought about another life lost another that stood waiting the unknown for another moment. To present day, today *'My boots'* the commentary was unfinished.

Standing before an audience, that was not a play, the congregation for a church, a rabbi, priest, the audience embodiment of organized collective casket seating, the bleachers brought about a future for the future stands. We hold to the strength, as the stand before us is unveiled, reactions not recorded only the findings, announced, delivered, presented- the bare of arms and bear of arms wave on to come forth, disperse not always in order – from a gun to a woven fabric combined simultaneously. Announcements made visual, unseen *'I didn't see it coming.' 'Extremities are missing.' 'Cold,' the commentary. 'Where are their rights?' 'In the written and displayed Bill- no play bill,' the commentary.*

'What's been written?' the commentary. The abacus started to multiply

beads of reign drops across an expansion that's not measurable in records, the non-mention- able to disable, misfire, back away at a line never visual in clear view that included the humanitarian. *Alice's in Wonder Land* was not a child's book read when the imposter of a fictional queen yelled for capital punishment- no one was in the looking glass on a print fictional page as the hue became the rain of the distraught tainted clearly of the body draining. The lady was put upon a pedestal as a self-appointment- it drained in another direction directing the attention finally to an identifiable one that channeled its way with a directive of one to be followed by all- the armor and its weapons were ordered months to days in advance before the path was announced to be taken serious as the abacus tallied to be attributed to the known taken on the order of a self-fulfilled destination- not a compliment for the humanitarian. The cold of the northern sky looked for new clothing to warm the son above they announced that had arrived in all. The pile was not a stack of wood. Wood refined to be written upon the page as a stench was aired for those that arrived. *'God bless you,' the commentary.* No complimentary flattering, absent of all hues, of gloss paper found to compliment a decorative living room wall as a pleasant reminder.

'When was the pinnacle?' 'Where's the pinnacle?' 'How long do you think it will last this time?' 'How do I get there?' 'Did I get close?' 'Do think I'll make?' the commentary. We stand at Arlington, VA cemetery. We held our breath as the hues in the sky may reflect the days. Thread that twined the days of a passing woman that was claimed to wove the fabric that went missing in conversation as the view held our breathe. Again, we're looking to recover a conversation with an arced cemented stone with more than the addressed listed. At our hands reach of placid flowers that never grew from the ground. The preservation of a memory held light was of the placing of a hunger that remained to tell, to explain the outcome of their participation. *'Walk with me,' the commentary.* A conversation only to a few that will walk, as they feel the grounded surface *'Maybe I should touch the grass that grows freely' 'What color changes in the fabric changed in design or was it the hues?' 'I'll keep you posted on my or our next arrival.' 'Who will be here next time with me?' 'They may be with you.' 'Don't look for an arrival to soon,' the commentary. 'Praying.'*

They aired Joe and Rose-founded the future at end. Two, aired of voice boomed exposed considered incidents that multiplied in an arc tally of future to multiply even more to a final destination lain to rest-hopeful perception of Joe to Rose. Arc lain before us in Arlington Cemetery, VA. Fore told end of the Cenozoic (Age of the Mammals and Man). The rest may not be of the passing told from the lain slain with appointed halos half arced in stone. It was the convincing conversations of a fore told love(s) turning another direction aired that was to enlighten the opposition with corrections that the heart was plotted in another negative directive. The perceptions and truth tested to a wait -cemented halos half arc continued to fulfill.

'A stand fully clothed with No cloths' the commentary. Lack of senses as one as many does not acknowledge a deity spirit in surround visually waiting the watched. A battle with destinations of those that plotted their feet look into each other- both looking for each other to become the cemented arc and a return to others for a Life. *'Not looking for a metal to turn to purple' the commentary.* LIFE FOR A LIFE- the Value is NOT written- a donation was a referral that both to live preferred as a LIFE FOR LIFE was to LIVE. 'If the backyard keeps a full view,' the commentary. 'We might make it pass to the goal,' the commentary.

Hearing a breathe that should not even be heard at inhale the exhale slowly expelled as nerves tighten the ropes that wraps the body visual to non-visual. Butterfly's before the anticipated grab held to a simulated stomach stayed to nature only as a metaphorical thought in displacement of historical moment of oneself – a rush of accelerants that generate the human body origin.

3rd *Chapter*

'A purple heart'

History commentary:

'The **Purple Heart Metal** was designed for all soldiers *wounded or killed* in war since 1782, the American Revolutionary War, applied to all branches of military.'

'Depending on second wounds resulting in a second metal, different metals for different branches are awarded in addition to the initial first *Purple Heart Metal* (only one *Purple Heart Metal* is given). Then in addition to the *Purple Heart Metal*, the *Oak Leaf Cluster* is assigned to U.S. Army and Airforce and the *Gold Star* is awarded for Navy, Marine and Coast Guard.'

Please take a moment to look, reflect upon your life as you view (pause, reflect) before you read *'Passed Away of a Sun'*...

4TH CHAPTER

Standing I've returned upon the ground that was once inhabited by animals and trees that held Fall as a season-not of man or woman. The trials could not be by gaveled by gravel fast enough- the parlor held the fancies for only a few in upper arrangement secretly to celebrate an achievement that may of included a tap into a vein or artery when death drained of the body to give it an after Life. Brass may of lived on with a memory of only a few that mistook a celebration for revealed justification for many that where not invited or could not attend-invitations sent for a double celebration only revealed to a few remaining- only a few arced in the future lain to rest in view when history told the news of a record demise- of what party attended by who or whom-the results? Toes held their names that night where the neck lain barren.

Measurement of time was it a waste of time? The remembrance of time treasured to look for a past to be recreated upon a celebrated holiday that did not include an uncomfortable past to reproduce for a forward. Coffee steamed over the fire. *'Purification of water was using a filter,'* the commentary. *'Cleaning your socks?'* the commentary. Ethics became a question with ethnics. *'Should I return the rainbow to keep the primary colors and get rid of the secondary or tertiary colors? 'the commentary.* Of God of a nature's palate all are welcome. 'Maybe a separation is welcome to a form a building strength,' the commentary of a future time of not of the same war. Of the first of the world, it was recorded as worldwide and the fight for humanitarians where to return to each country they chose to belong they called home.

'Throw it on the Pyle,' the commentary. *'What's the pile?'* the commentary. Paper, logs, sticks, hay, flesh... .Humanitarian's peaked an interest. Erine wasn't just a way to get a pay check. The bill did not pass until it was written. The ten of an oblong rectangle representation in a number was posted in result to a written epic of a true tale to each military personnel's personal monthly allowance. *'What was written?'* the commentary. *'There's a ten in the account,'* the commentary. *'What was written?'* the commentary. [1]

Mass numbered a measurement in weight, concentration, form- also measured the number-atomic, particle(s), vapors then people. There was a positive charge from a uniform equivalent- the equation changed as charges where charged. *'They dug the hole deep enough for many,'* the commentary. *'I think they dug it for themselves,'* the commentary. With the winds that carried an upper draft – was it written for themselves? The equation crossed the upper draft

---

[1] Question in history – Who was the famous journalist and his history? Here you will find the answer to both questions, the paragraph questions written in footnote. Answer on toward back of the book on closing commentary. (This paragraph was inserted in honor of my nephew Robert (Paulie) Griffiths who passed away that loved to read history. The journalist was one of his favorites. At the age of 10 years old, my nephew acquired a sense of what life was about while reading the journalist books on WW II. He understood the compassion that the journalist wrote about of the conditions that the soldiers lived through. – God rest and bless my nephew's soul as well as the journalist who helped him see the compassion of a human to other humans written on paper.)

for the first to be concentrated-it warmed the first of the world then warmed it further the second time. *'No chamber maid in a fairytale,' the commentary.* The castle became the dreaded dungeon. *'Don't breath in,' the commentary. 'Grab the mask, ' the commentary.* Thee contained did not have a mask. *'Pray, 'the commentary.*

4th Chapter

History commentary:

Ethnic cleansing is forced removal of ethnics from a country(s) out of one or more countries – it may include mass murder.

There is more than one reason that a war happens. This along with technology advancements of combat artillery mixed with political and economic values that include changes.

In 1915, WWI **Chlorine gas** was one of the technology advancements used in combat artillery weapons. It was the first time used in war for this gas.

Please take a moment to look, reflect upon your life as you view (pause, reflect) before you read *Passed Away of a Sun*...

5TH CHAPTER

The days of passing they numbered the calendar. *'I counted the days here,'* the commentary. *'Has it been a year?'* the commentary. *'Longer..'the* commentary that was not finished but interrupted.

God granted the sun to shine, to set, only the numbering was confused with the weather for those that did not keep track. Stand before the arced placed in stone on many a day looking out into what, who or why. *'I prefer to be here with you,'* the commentary. *'They did not chose to take the ride to talk with you today,'* the commentary. *'Only I did- I chose to stand before you now just for this moment today,'* the commentary. *'My wedding is with you,'* the commentary. *'I arrived watching you,'* the commentary. *'Do I turn to see who is behind me?'* the commentary. *'The winds have taken on a different toll of direction or who directed me to you,'* the commentary. *'Should I turn to see who is behind me,'* the commentary.

Arms that hold are not who they thought would ever hold them. The silver crafted around braced wrists that made a place on some that took the journey of an end they thought they could out playout in the end. The summons arrived. A hopeful right of judgement- handing off the bill.

Operative was a definition that was used in all wars. The steel rods of thin refined glass to a pole broke...- a man's extremities where affected as well as a functional expel of a fine yellow distain liquid that should never been affected by a shatter of refined glass. *'What the hell where you after?' the commentary. 'Location,' the commentary.*

'Take hold of my hand and follow me,' the commentary. A parent's nightmare was to grab back what his and his wife held onto for the nine months for life to exist on. *'Go on take the papers with you,' the commentary.* No last hug only a remembrance of watching them walk away. A push of stiffness filled the air as the smoke rolled black in puffs from the coaled engine that roved the tracks. Crowded with confusion as limited room filled with hugs of shoulder to shoulder the same age or similar where arms were not holding an embrace of an already known- they were cleaning only in the wrong order and not for God. The gas was released. *'Who's watched?' the commentary.*

'Hold it,' the commentary strong with force heard from the wrong hoped for the eventually the right of a bill. A bucket, a separate space or place to relieve natural fluid of a body so that the body can cleanse it's self naturally became the plea bargain in the beginning. *'Please.....'the commentary.* The bus was not held or stopped. A decision for a bucket never left the front of the bus. 'Fear' separated them from their country. They came to put their future in planting their roots many years before- roots where pulled-the harbor know for a pearl held the bottom that rooted them. A penitentiary was made to hold a group that was found innocent/guilty due to a ruined harbor. The yellow of a bus did not match the flag they up-rooted at the time-looking for an orange sun of fabric symbolism-both flew the same flag- the guilt/innocent, innocent/guilt, guilt and the innocent.[2]

'Stand unclothed,' the commentary. Artic water encased in a wooden drawn bucket held their stature closed behind a closet door. *'Looking for eye color to change,' the commentary.* Chatter of a shiver that never left the bone-skeletal walked without the metal hinges of a biology lab. Poland was not warm only on a paper as a doctor that took notes to make the perfected. Still it was born became two- even as the feet tied as well as knees held the legs held the host- death

---

[2] *Internment of Japanese Americans* forced relocation and incarceration for 110,000 and 120,000 Japanese Americans per the order of President Roosevelt by due to Japan's attack on Pearl Harbor December 7, 1941. Pearl Harbor death total 188 U.S. aircraft were destroyed; 2,403 Americans were killed.

departed both. *'Only a pain measurement,'* the commentary. *'Made the note,'* the commentary. *'Files presented after the war,'* the commentary. *'Did you find them yourself?'* the commentary.[3]

'What was the right of passage?' the commentary. Last rites where given only to those that had the request fulfilled by an honored stand in for the pulpit without chapel in sight. Where the church bells rang only if there was a strong enough wind that the storm brewed during the day or night. A fight for the age to get old enough to hold the gun they carried- the adults were becoming scarce – 13 was the average number that became the norm for a halted walk that never became a walking bands march to hoist the draft of a wind that blew too far and too hard in the front of them. *'Biscuit'* the commentary. *'Biscuit?'* the commentary. *'He should have been school,'* the commentary. *'Lay the jacket over him,'* the commentary. The cold warmed-not – the look of the warm needed to be warmed to prevent the cold of a mistake. The jacket stayed cold underneath-the arced was in view. *'He should have been in school,'* the commentary repeated. *'Biscuit?'* the commentary.

5th Chapter

History commentary:

Bill of Rights was first ten amendments of the Constitution that was passed by congress and ratified (activated in written status) December 15, 1791 under the United States President George Washington.

The **Universal Declaration of Human Rights** drafted by representatives of the all countries in the United Nations proclaimed by the United Nations December 10 1948. First document to protect human rights all over the world. The president of the United States at that time was President Theodore Roosevelt. WW II ended December 1946. Two years after WWII ended.

---

[3] Topic: Freezing / Hypothermia experiments done at Dachau, Article title: Nazi Scientists and Ethics of Today, New York Times,1989, May 21, http://www.nytimes.com/1989/05/21/us/nazi-scientists-and-ethics-of-today.html?pagewanted=all Human Experimentation, Chapter 7 Section 4. Readings: Book title 'The Ethical Considerations of Medical Exon Human Subjects' Manny Bekier, M.S. November 18, 2010

ADDITIONAL HISTORY POETRY COMMENTARY BY THE AUTHOR

The world is represented and visually sought in Arlington National Cemetery, Arlington, Virginia, United States.

For many that passed on due to war that lay in Arlington National Cemetery, the rising of a sunshine day in many people lives that included their parents, care givers, etc. died the day those that were placed in the ground. Many never found happiness again, not on earth when until they passed. Many moved forward happy that their life was some way affected by those that they met- hopefully an improvement.

'Passed Away of the Sun' was named with 'Sun' not 'Son' to show **respect** to Christians, Jews and Muslims that believe in Jesus Christ as God or a prophet in a religious manner. And **respect** to those that are dead and buried in Arlington National Cemetery and those that been affected by war (all war) that the sun of a sunshine day passed away from many lives on earth when they passed away in war (all war). They were NOT Jesus Christ at end.

The world in the arced grave stone. Please close the gates at Arlington National Cemetery with a sign on the front gate in the future with *'Completely full! Peace be with you!'* *'May all war end and spilt milk prevail!*

Carol Lee Brunk
November 30, 2015

NOTES

<u>NOTES</u>

NOTES

NOTES

<u>*NOTES*</u>